TEEN MENTAL HEALTH™

meditation

Andrew Moore

ROSEN
PUBLISHING

New York

Published in 2009 by The Rosen Publishing Group, Inc.
29 East 21st Street, New York, NY 10010

First Edition

Library of Congress Cataloging-in-Publication Data

Moore, Andrew.
Meditation / Andrew Moore.
    p. cm.—(Teen mental health)
Includes bibliographical references and index.
ISBN-13: 978-1-4042-1799-7 (library binding)
1. Meditation—Juvenile literature. 2. Teenagers—Conduct of life—Juvenile literature. I. Title.
BF637.M4M66 2009
158.1'2—dc22

                                            2008013567

Manufactured in the United States of America

contents

chapter one   What Is Meditation? **4**

chapter two   Learning the Practice of
                Meditation **7**

chapter three   Contemplation, Chanting,
                and Mantras **17**

chapter four   The Ancient Origins of
                Meditation **21**

chapter five   Meditation and Your Life **30**

glossary   **42**

for more information   **44**

for further reading   **46**

index   **47**

chapter one

What Is Meditation?

Meditation is listening to the Divine within.
—Edgar Cayce

You may have had a stressful day recently and wondered to yourself, "Is this all there is to life?" You might have had an argument with a friend or parent and felt like you just needed some breathing room. Or, you may have a big sports competition or piano recital coming up, and might be worried that your nerves will get in your way. If you're stuck, stressed, or just looking for a bit of fresh air in your life, meditation may be the relief you're seeking.

You have probably seen pictures of celebrities such as Madonna or Richard Gere sitting cross-legged in meditation. In history class, you may learn about the Indian leader Mahatma Gandhi using meditation as part of his nonviolent plan to liberate India from British rule. Perhaps while watching television you have seen the Dalai Lama from Tibet, in his saffron and yellow robes, and you have heard that he practices the art of meditation.

You may be wondering what meditation is. Maybe you are a seeker, someone who looks for ways to make your life happier and more balanced. Or, you may be a very active person who wonders why anyone would want to practice meditation because it appears to be a waste of time. Maybe you have already tried meditation techniques and you want additional information.

Meditation is a broad subject. There are many different methods and styles of meditation: from exercises in which you sit

Silent prayer and contemplation are just two of the many forms of meditation.

5

very still, to methods based on movement, to visual meditations used for sports and other activities. There are just as many reasons why people try meditation. Some of these reasons may include gaining inner happiness and peace of mind, improving a sense of health and spirituality, reducing the body's level of stress and anxiety, or becoming a more disciplined and focused individual.

Meditation is a tool that an individual can use to help understand his or her body, mind, and spirit. It can bring insight, peace, and energy to any man, woman, teen, or child. Those who suffer from borderline personality disorder, a mental health condition that causes someone to be very anxious and carried away by thoughts, can find great relief through the practice of meditation. The experience of mindfulness, being present with one's moment-to-moment experience, is a powerful antidote to anxiety. Everyone has access to the power of meditation.

Meditation can be different for everyone, and it is usually a very individualized experience. For many, meditation allows a person to bypass the daily chatter of the mind to connect with his or her inner self.

chapter two

Learning the Practice of Meditation

We are what we think. All that we are arises with our thoughts.
                    —The Buddha

There are common misconceptions about meditation. Some people think you have to go to a monastery or to another religious place to meditate. The truth is that anyone can meditate anywhere and at any time. Other people are concerned that meditating might conflict with their religious beliefs. But at its heart, meditation is about cultivating peace of mind and an open attitude toward one's life, not about adopting a particular religion. While meditation is often practiced as part of Eastern religions, like Buddhism or Hinduism, it is not at all necessary to change your religious beliefs in order to meditate.

The simple act of meditation is an internal act of cultivating the mind and is often called mindfulness. In the words of the Buddha, "Meditation untangles what is

Buddhism has a long tradition of meditation. These Buddhist monks are meditating at Borobudur, an Indonesian shrine built in the eighth or ninth century CE.

tangled." Many people equate the idea of meditation with a concentrated level of spiritual consciousness. To meditate is to look beneath the fabric of our thoughts and allow the sense of inner peace and oneness that is deep within us to surface. Some people find that practicing meditation helps heal the body, sharpen the mind, and rejuvenate the spirit. For many others, meditation serves as a simple practice to provide relief from stress and anxiety because of its ability to easily calm the mind.

Calming the Mind

The paths to meditation are varied, but they have at least one common goal: calming the mind. Whether you are a Tibetan monk, an African tribal holy man, an athlete using visualization to improve a high jump, or a beginning yoga student, the first goal of meditation is to calm, or stabilize, the mind. Calming the mind can be achieved simply by sitting still, closing the eyes, and resting your attention on the breath.

You are taught to calm the mind by resting it on an object of meditation, for example, the breath, or an imagined image. If your mind strays away from the object of meditation toward other distracting thoughts, you should gently bring it back to its point of origin.

Meditation Exercise No. 1: Calming the Mind

In the following calming-the-mind meditation, you will use your breath as the object of the meditation. The breath is always with us but is always changing, so it is a wonderful starting place for meditation. Try the practice below for five minutes. Over time, you may want to increase your meditation session to ten or even twenty minutes, but five is good to start.

1. Sit in a comfortable position, in a chair or cross-legged on the floor. Let your hands rest on your legs.
2. Close your eyes and let your attention rest on the breath. You don't have to breathe any more deeply than normal—just be with your breathing as it is.
3. If thoughts come into your mind as you breathe, don't try to stop them or focus on them. Just say to yourself "thinking," and gently bring your mind back to the breath.

Developing a Meditation Practice

If you tried the meditation exercise above, you have taken the first step toward developing a daily meditation practice. To develop a practice, it helps to meditate every day. A new practitioner might set five or ten minutes a day as a reasonable goal for his or her meditation practice. However, the most important thing is not the length of time for which you meditate; the most important part of developing a practice is to aim for something you can do every day, even if it's just a few minutes. Some people meditate for twenty minutes, twice per day. During days when you cannot do your full practice, you can still meditate for one or two minutes. By keeping a regular schedule, you develop stability in your body and mind,

Meditation is not complicated. If you are a beginner, simply sit in a comfortable position with your eyes closed and focus on your breathing.

and the benefits of meditation will be available to you whenever you need them.

Your Meditation Environment

Generally, it is a good idea to find a quiet place in which to meditate. Find a convenient place, inside or outside, that you can devote to your daily practice. Arrange objects

This Japanese monk is meditating in a rock garden. The peaceful environment is ideal for maintaining concentration.

around your special area that put you at ease, like fragrant candles or incense, pictures of mentors or spiritual guides, or objects such as flowers, rocks, or shells that are inspirational to you. Meditating outdoors in a natural setting, like near a lake, can also be inspiring if the spot is private and secluded.

Timekeeping During Meditation

Monitoring the passage of time with a clock or watch during your daily meditation practice is helpful so that you can meditate more freely and not worry about being late for school or dinner because of your practice. Another timekeeping technique is to record the instructions for your favorite meditation on a cassette tape or to use a timer. Many people choose a specific time of day to meditate such as in the morning or just before bed. The morning hours, when the mind is refreshed from a good night's sleep, are said to be the best for meditating. Everyone is different, though, and you may find that other times work better for you.

Finding Your Comfortable Meditation Position

When many people think of the art of meditation, they imagine someone sitting in the lotus position, in which the feet are brought to rest on the thighs in a cross-legged fashion. But while sitting in the full or half-lotus position or simply sitting cross-legged with the hands resting on the knees is generally the style in yoga and Zen meditations, it is not necessary to remain in any position that is uncomfortable in order to meditate. Cushions and stools can also be used to make sitting cross-legged more comfortable, or meditation can be done sitting in a chair. Occasionally, meditations are even done lying down.

Solitary or Group Meditation

Finally, you can meditate alone or in a group during a meditation class. Some people find that they like the

For sitting meditation, it's important to find a posture that you can maintain without discomfort.

feeling of the group's energy. Others prefer the solace that solitary meditation provides.

Becoming Aware of Your Thoughts

Sometimes, people experience negative or limiting thoughts without even being aware of them. These thoughts are playing over and over in the background of our minds, like faintly audible music. Sometimes, it is easy to just let go of these thoughts, but other times we might find that they have more power over us. Helpful or harmful, we cannot always control the thoughts that come into our minds. However, the practice of meditation can cultivate a more positive outlook on life, and we can often find ourselves unexpectedly happy. Even when our thoughts are dark and stormy, meditating can give us a deeper insight into our true feelings. In this way, meditation can be a powerful tool for awakening confidence and compassion.

Just as the sky can be full of clouds, the mind can be full of all sorts of thoughts. Meditation helps us move our attention from these cloud-like surface thoughts and rest in the sky-like peace and intelligence behind them. You can try to shift your focus like this even when you're not meditating. At times when you are confused or upset, take a moment to breathe in and out, and notice how your body feels. Try to experience the "big sky" mind behind your thoughts. A five-second time-out like this can be a great way to bring some fresh air into a tough day.

15

Ten Great Questions to Ask a Meditation Specialist

1. How often do I need to meditate in order to feel less stressed?

2. I'm interested in Buddhism or Hinduism. Can you recommend some books?

3. I'm not interested in Hinduism or Buddhism. Will meditation still help me?

4. Can you help me bring meditation into my sports practice/ music practice/daily life?

5. Do I have to practice meditation sitting cross-legged in a quiet place, like I've seen people do on TV?

6. What is the background of this particular tradition? How long has your meditation center been in operation?

7. The meditation centers here seem to be full of adults. Are there any groups for teenagers who like to meditate?

8. I've been doing yoga for a while now. How can I incorporate the practice of meditation into my yoga poses?

9. I'm originally from a Christian/Jewish/Muslim tradition. How can I combine meditation with my own faith?

10. Can I expect meditation to help me with my relationships/ schoolwork/difficulty sleeping?

chapter three

Contemplation, Chanting, and Mantras

Sometimes, people use words and sounds as the objects of meditation. The words may be a phrase such as "May all people everywhere be happy," or "May all people everywhere be free from suffering." Meditating on phrases like these is known as contemplation practice. Contemplation practice is a way to cultivate inner peace and kindness.

Some meditators will also chant, or recite, the words of a text from their tradition as part of their daily practice. Repeating the words of ancient teachers and meditators can illuminate your experience of a practice and bring a bit of ancient wisdom into your daily life. Over time, people find that the meanings of these profound chants speak to their lives in deep and personal ways that they did not understand when they first heard the words.

Mantras

Words may be chanted for their sound, rather than their meaning, in which case they are known as mantras. The vibrations of the sound create a resonance in the body. Mantras are based on this physical vibration. For some, mantras are prayers or sacred thoughts.

The actual word "mantra" is derived from a phrase in the ancient Indian language of Sanskrit meaning "a tool of thought." According to Sogyal Rinpoche, in his book *The Tibetan Book of Living and Dying*, "Each syllable [of the mantra] is impregnated with spiritual power. Each condenses a spiritual truth and vibrates with a blessing. When you chant a mantra, you are charging your breath and energy with the energy of that mantra."

Meditation Exercise No. 2: Mantra Chanting

Om Mani Padme Hum (pronounced "ohm mah nee pahd may hum") is both a Hindu and a Buddhist mantra of compassion. Chanting it is said to enhance your positive feelings toward all things.

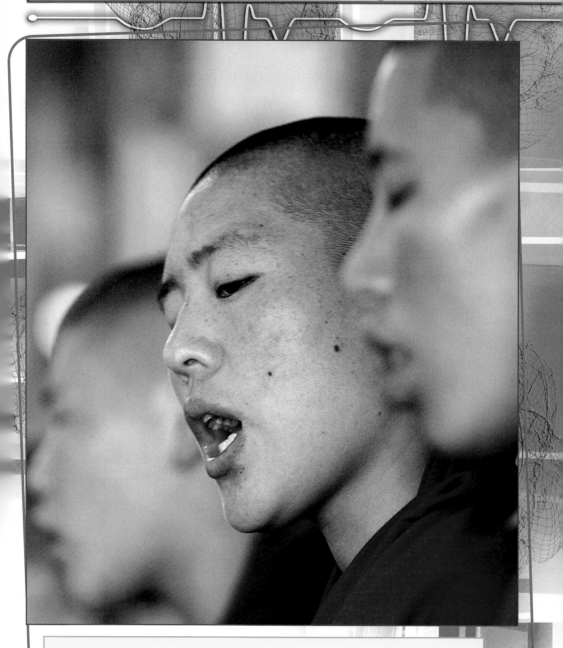

Buddhist nuns in Kathmandu, Nepal, meditate during *puja*, a special type of chanting prayer.

1. Sit in a comfortable position. Close your eyes. Let your attention rest on the breath.
2. Bring to mind a positive wish you might have for the world, like, "May there be peace on Earth."
3. Begin repeating the mantra *Om Mani Padme Hum.* Continue repeating this mantra for five minutes.
4. Sit in silence. Notice the calming effects of the chanting.

Meditation Exercise No. 3: Contemplating Kindness

The contemplation of kindness is a basic practice in many meditative traditions. This exercise begins with you wishing happiness for yourself, then for a friend, and finally for all people and animals everywhere.

1. Sit in a comfortable position and allow the mind to rest on the breath until you feel calm and ready to begin.
2. Now say to yourself silently, "May I be happy." Allow your mind to rest in that phrase for a few moments. If you find your attention wandering, simply bring your attention back to the phrase.
3. Now bring to mind a friend, family member, or pet that you feel affectionate toward. Think, "May [this person or animal] be happy."
4. Finally, wish happiness to all people and animals everywhere: "May all beings be happy."

chapter four

The Ancient Origins of Meditation

Now that you have tried some meditations, you may want to know something about the ancient origins of this practice.

Meditation Practices in the East

Eastern philosophies share the belief in the interconnectedness of all things and all people. Two major traditions, which have their origins in India, are Buddhism and Hinduism. The traditions share many similarities, but differ on some key philosophical

This giant statue of the meditating Buddha is located atop Bagua Mountain, in Changhua, Taiwan.

points. They both emphasize meditation, however.

Buddhism

The central figure of Buddhism, the Buddha, was born a prince named Siddhartha in a kingdom in the foothills of the Himalayas in 563 BCE. When he was twenty-nine, he became very concerned with the suffering of the people in his country and set out to find a solution. He tried all of the spiritual paths that were available in an effort to discover why people suffer. Still, he did not find the answers he was seeking.

Finally, after meditating for forty-nine days, he realized the answers to all his questions. According to the story, he experienced complete enlightenment and became known by the Sanskrit word "Buddha," which means "one who is awake." Later, the Buddha taught others how to seek peace through meditation and other teaching methods. At the same time, he told his students to seek out the truth for themselves, rather than follow a teacher blindly. His methods of teaching became known as Buddhism—which literally means "Awake-ism." These teachings became

22

very widespread in Asian countries and today are practiced by people all over the world.

The goal of many Buddhists is to cultivate complete awareness, acceptance, and openness to all thoughts, situations, and people. If they can do this consistently and maintain a peaceful mind, then they have attained enlightenment, or "nirvana." Nirvana is not a place, like heaven in the Christian belief system. It is also not an extraordinary, "high" feeling. Instead, it has been described as a deep understanding of and appreciation for life. Someone who has attained enlightenment will most likely radiate a feeling of complete peace and comfort.

Zen Buddhism began in India and spread to China and then Japan. The aim of this sect of Buddhism is to reach enlightenment by practicing a combination of sitting meditation and contemplation of "koans," traditional riddles that a teacher assigns to a student. (One famous koan is: "What is the sound of one hand clapping?") The late, legendary conductor of the Berlin Philharmonic Orchestra, Herbert von Karajan, was a dedicated practitioner of Zen Buddhism. You can get a sense of his spacious, precise style by watching *2001: A Space Odyssey*. Von Karajan conducted the opening title music "Also Sprach Zarathustra" and the music for "Travel to The Moon," more familiarly known as "On the Beautiful Blue Danube."

Buddhism also spread to Tibet. Tibetan Buddhism often uses visualization, a form of meditation in which one imagines scenes and images in the mind during meditation. In one Tibetan-Buddhist meditation, for instance, destructive thoughts of hatred, anger, and jealousy are replaced with thoughts of love and compassion.

These people are performing early-morning tai chi exercises in Kunming, Yunnan Province, China.

China developed forms of meditative exercises such as tai chi, believed to bring mental, physical, and spiritual benefits to those who practice it. Likewise, the martial arts of the East, based on various fighting skills and movements, also have a meditative component.

Hinduism

Hinduism, the other major religion of India, is actually a very diverse faith with no one teacher or god that is universally worshipped. However, Brahman, who is sometimes described as a god and sometimes as the universal energy of the soul, is revered and said to pervade all things. Some Hindus also honor other gods such as Shiva, Krishna, or Rama. Like Buddhists, Hindus believe that the entire physical and spiritual worlds are united and that all things are interconnected.

Yoga, a meditation path associated with Hinduism, is an approach with specific techniques for achieving the peace of mind inherent in the experience of oneness. Today, the practice of yoga is widespread in the Western world. Many health clubs offer classes in yoga, which focuses the mind through a system of physical postures called asanas. These postures are said to have beneficial effects on the internal organs and on one's state of mind.

Meditation Practices in the West

In the late 1960s and 1970s, there was a deep divide in the United States. Many young people rebelled against the traditions and culture of their parents and the politicians in power. It

In the United States, the ancient art of yoga is often practiced as part of an exercise and fitness regimen.

was a time of great social change when the civil rights movement and the anti–Vietnam War movement sparked conflict and confrontation. At this time of openness and change, many people were inspired to look beyond traditional Western religions. An Indian guru named Maharishi Yogi (1917–2008) introduced a meditation practice called transcendental meditation that was attractive to Westerners in its simplicity and its reputation for providing inner peace. Even earlier, Swiss psychiatrist Carl Jung (1875–1961) had begun using visualization with his clients. Since then, many people have taken up meditation in the West. This is

Whirling dervishes are Sufi mystics of the Turkish Mevlevi Order. Here, they perform their hypnotic Sema ceremony.

sometimes referred to as New Age meditation, although many of the techniques being taught are very old.

Some Western religious traditions have offshoots with a meditative side. All Judaism, Christianity, and Islamic meditation take the form of prayer. In the mystical branch of Judaism that teaches the Kabbalah, the seeker hopes to transcend the mundane and experience the divine. To do this, seekers are inspired through guided meditation techniques. Some of these techniques parallel methods found in Zen Buddhism. In Sufism, a mystical branch of Islam, prayers take the form of dance. Sufis whirl for long periods of time while repeating sacred phrases and the name of the deity to achieve oneness with the divine.

Meditation in North and South America

The meditation techniques used by the indigenous people of North and South America stretch back for centuries. Although the specific meditative practices vary from culture to culture, traditional North American Native Americans see spirits in all living things and see themselves as a part of nature. According to this tradition, the trees, rocks, animals, wind, rain, clouds, and human beings all have an inner spirit. It is possible to speak to all of them through the act of ceremony. In their worldview, all natural phenomena are part of a spiritual continuum, which must be in balance in order to survive. Traditionally, many North American Native Americans use their dances as a moving meditation, in which prayers are sent via the feet to honor the earth and create universal harmony.

MYTHS AND FACTS

Myth: Meditation—isn't that a way to get away from all the stresses of life?

Fact: Meditation can be a great help in dealing with stressful or upsetting situations, but it is not a way of running from them. It encourages us to take a calm, compassionate look at our lives and find a way to move forward with a peace of mind.

Myth: Meditation is a religious activity, practiced by members of Asian religious sects.

Fact: While many Asian religions such as Buddhism and Hinduism support the practice of meditation as part of their belief system, their members are far from being the world's only meditators! Meditation itself is just a simple human act of becoming awake to one's thoughts and feelings. People all over the world, in every religion, practice meditation.

Myth: Meditation is going to make me a more boring, less fun person. What will my friends think?

Fact: Meditation can calm you down, but it usually doesn't make people become hermits or act any less cool. The people who meditate for years and years usually have very distinct, juicy personalities because they are not afraid to be real. In fact, you may become just the breath of fresh air that your friends are looking for!

Myth: If I meditate and visualize really well, my problems will go away.

Fact: Unfortunately, this is not true. However, engaging with the problems of your life with a calm, alert mind and a positive, caring attitude has been known to make a difference for the better!

Myth: The Buddha said that everything is full of suffering. How can it be that a famous meditator such as him had such a "down" outlook on things?

Fact: The Buddha didn't exactly say that everything is full of suffering. What he said was that life goes up and down, but that things are always changing, and that the basic fabric of our life is good. He saw that it was possible to live with an awakened heart and an intelligent mind through all the ups and downs of life.

Myth: I'm having a really hard time right now, and I'm feeling anxious and depressed. Is meditation the solution?

Fact: Meditation might help you get some clarity about your feelings, but if you are overwhelmed or are having very strong feelings, speaking to a counselor or trusted adult is a better place to start. Remember, the Buddha found that life is a basically good experience and that we all can achieve happiness.

chapter five

Meditation and Your Life

The spirits told me if a bad thought or bad word ever comes to you, to let it go in your ear and out the other ear, but never out your mouth. If it comes out of your mouth, it is going to hurt somebody and then that hurt will come back to you twice.
—Wallace H. Black Elk

Meditation is not just an intrinsic part of the philosophies of some of the major world religions; it is also a powerful aid for living your life in a way that is fulfilling and fun. Meditation can be used to approach specific situations or problems with confidence, clarity, and compassion.

Affirmations

An affirmation is a positive phrase that you can create as an aid in overcoming difficulty or to enhance your life. An affirmation on any subject is always stated in a positive way. For instance, an affirmation statement could be, "I get good grades in math class," rather than, "I won't fail in math class." State affirmations in the present tense, like, "My courage is increasing," rather than, "I will try to be less fearful."

A good time to create powerful affirmations for your-self is when you are not feeling your best. When something is upsetting you, try to discover the thoughts behind the emotions you are feeling. Then you have the raw material necessary to create a truthful and useful affirmation.

For example, if you feel anxious while waiting to hear about a college application, you may be thinking, "I'll never get into college." Create an affirmation that says the opposite: "I am accepted into the school that is right for me."

Reciting affirmations won't solve all of your problems, but it can help you stay upbeat when you are dealing with a difficult situation.

Or, if you have applied for a job and are fearful of not getting it, say, "I will have the perfect job for me." If you are always tongue-tied and embarrassed in social situations, you can create several affirmations such as, "People enjoy speaking with me," "I am a good listener," and, "People value my company."

Affirmations activate the subconscious mind to create better thought patterns. By repeating positive, affirmative statements of the results we seek to create, a wealth of favorable information is reinforced in our minds.

The following are several basic affirmations:

- I deserve love, happiness, and success.
- I respect and love my body.
- I am a beautiful creation of the universe, and I am loved and valued for just being myself.

Never create phrases that seek to harm others. Always create affirmations about yourself and about ideas and thought patterns that you want to change, rather than about other people you may want to change.

Affirmations help us think positively, build our confidence, and help us to develop faith in ourselves and our lives. Whenever you are facing a challenge, ask yourself: How can I do this? Where can I get help? What is the outcome I want to create? Then, create some affirmations that state your goals as if they have already happened.

First, create the affirmation you want to use, like, "I am a successful student." Use that phrase while meditating morning and night for twenty-one days. The repetition of working with an affirmation impresses the positive way of thinking on the mind's subconscious. It is in that way that you will begin to see positive changes.

During the day, if doubts and insecurities arise such as negative thought patterns, substitute your affirmative thoughts for the negative ideas. If you need to, refer to your affirmation by writing it down and carrying it with you. Be alert to all the ways in which your new affirmation is affecting your life.

Meditation Exercise No. 4: Affirmation Meditation

This exercise will help you work with affirmations in a very direct and simple way. You may want to start by quietly focusing on the breath for two or three minutes. When you are ready, begin the exercise below.

1. Sit in a comfortable position. Close your eyes and focus your mind, creating a feeling of calmness. Breathe slowly and deeply three times.

2. Now repeat your affirmation, either silently or aloud, twenty-one times. Allow yourself to believe that the affirmation is already true. Say it with energy and enthusiasm. If your mind presents you with any reason why this cannot be true, gently lead it back to your original affirmation statement.

3. Finish your meditation with three slow, deep breaths. Open your eyes and sit silently for a few moments.

Specific Meditations

Many find that deep, prolonged thought with specific meditations is a great way to relieve mental or emotional pain.

For many people, the act of meditation is useful for minimizing stress and anxiety, reducing pain, and achieving a calmer state of mind. Other people use daily meditation exercises to deal with specific problems or troubling times in their lives that require a greater sense of concentration. The following meditations are meant to serve as specific instructions for you to follow. They will help you to develop increased mental focus, which can clear your mind of any uncertain thoughts.

Meditation Exercise No. 5: Creative Visualization for Success in Athletics

Like most achievements, competing in sporting events and activities takes control, grace, stamina, endurance, and concentration. Phil Jackson, a professional basketball coach for "dream teams" such as the Chicago Bulls and the L.A. Lakers, believes in the power of meditation. He has written about his mindful approach to the game and to leadership in his first book, *Sacred Hoops: Spiritual Lessons of a Hardwood Warrior*. Meditation is one way to help you achieve top form as an athletic competitor.

1. Sit or lie in a comfortable position. Imagine each section of your body relaxing. Ease any tension by doing a quick body scan, beginning in your toes and traveling through your body to the top of your head. As you check in with each section of your body, try to release any tension you may be holding.

2. Next, focus your awareness with three deep breaths.

3. Now put yourself in the setting of the sports activity. Vividly imagine the place, colors, lights, teammates, and spectators.

4. With an imaginary camera, zoom in on yourself. See yourself performing as a top athlete in peak form. If you have a sports goal that you want to reach, like jumping a certain distance or running a mile within a set amount of time, imagine yourself achieving that goal. Visualize yourself performing every detail. For instance, if it's a team sport, imagine hitting a home run, scoring the deciding goal, or catching the fly ball that wins the game.

5. Now use your camera to focus inside yourself. This camera can peer inside to your feelings and sensations. It prints out a message, like a ticker tape, that tells you all the feelings and sensations that are associated with reaching this goal that you have set for yourself. Focus deeply on those feelings.

6. In one graceful movement, stretch your arms out and bring all your feelings back inside yourself.

Return to your normal state of consciousness. Open your eyes. Sit for a moment and relax in your affirmative state, understanding that you are on your way to greater success.

Meditation Exercise No. 6: Creative Visualization for Freedom from Fear

We all experience fear. Fear is useful when it warns us of danger, but very often, fear stops us from doing things we would like to do. When fear stands in your way, try the following meditation.

1. Sit in a comfortable, quiet place. Close your eyes. Calm your mind, taking three deep breaths.
2. Now focus your attention on the inner sensations of your body. Imagine that you are searching your entire body, noting where the feelings of fear are located in your body.
3. Next, visualize just one of the places in your body where you sense fear exists. Ask yourself: If this fear were an object, what would it be? Does it have a shape, texture, or form?
4. It's time to examine your fear. Ask yourself: What is this fear about? What is it related to?
5. Now imagine a vast sky above you, with many clouds of all shapes and sizes floating past. Pause. Imagine that your fear is one of those clouds, and behind it is the vast sky, which has so much room. Now think that your mind is like the vast sky, all-embracing in its wisdom, compassion, and

confidence. Allow the cloud of fear to float through that vast sky of mind, aware that your strength and kindness are greater than that fear. Rest for a moment in the sky-like quality of your mind.

6.   Finish the exercise with a chant, affirmation, or prayer of your choice such as, "May all people enjoy freedom from fear."

Meditation Exercise No. 7: Breathing to Reduce Stress

The following breathing exercise is very calming and greatly reduces anxiety and stress. If you find it difficult to breathe out for eight counts, begin by breathing out for only three counts, and gradually increase the length of your exhale each time.

Begin this stress-reducing meditation practice by lying on a bed or a mat on the floor. Rest your hands on your abdomen.

1.   Close your eyes and focus inward.

Meditation exercises can give you a more positive outlook on things, while also contributing to your overall good health.

2. Take slow, relaxing breaths through your nostrils for the count of three seconds. Breathe deeply, filling your abdomen with air. Exhale gently out through the mouth for eight seconds.

3. Focus on the counting of each set of breaths. If your mind wanders, attempt to bring it back into focus. Concentrate only on controlled breathing.

4. Repeat this breathing exercise fifteen times.

5. Remain relaxed and silent for as long as possible. Open your eyes. Return to your activities with a renewed and calm energy.

Meditation Exercise No. 8: Dealing with Difficult People

In this meditation, you have the opportunity to send positive energy to people who are angry, bothersome, or downright irritating. Why is it helpful to send positive thoughts to your enemies? Simply, it will give you peace of mind from angry thoughts. Sometimes, it even transforms your relationship with that person.

Sit in a comfortable position. Close your eyes and relax your body.

1. Breathe deeply three times. Silently repeat these three phrases three times: "May I be happy," "May I be healthy," "May I be safe."

2. Now picture someone you look up to: a mentor, friend, or teacher. Say the same three phrases three more times for that person. "May she be happy," "May she be healthy," "May she be safe."

3. Next, picture someone you don't know. For instance, imagine someone you saw on the street and again say the same three phrases for them three times.

4. Now turn your attention to the difficult person in your life. As sincerely as you can, say the phrases three times for this person.

5. Finish by repeating the three phrases again for yourself.

6. Sit quietly for a few moments. Notice how you feel. Finish your meditation with three slow, deep breaths. Open your eyes. Relax.

A Day of Joy and Wisdom

People who meditate sometimes go on retreats so they can concentrate on meditating without the distractions of daily life. While at the retreat, they spend the whole day performing different kinds of meditation such as sitting meditation, walking meditation, chanting, or breathing exercises. They aspire to remain in a state of mindfulness all day and all night. You and your friends might try your own mini-retreat by doing the following practices on a day devoted entirely to meditation.

Meditation Exercise No. 9: Walking Meditation

In many meditation practices people are encouraged to be active, as in this exercise, where the objective of the meditation is the movement of walking. You should try to find a serene outdoor setting for this exercise.

1. Stand still and become aware of your entire body. As thoughts arise, tell yourself that you will gently return your focus to your body's own movement.
2. Begin moving slowly. Focus on the action of picking up your feet and putting them down.
3. Walk five or ten minutes along a path, and then turn and return to where you started.
4. Stand motionless for a moment and notice how you feel. Try to keep that feeling with you for the rest of the day.

Labyrinths are ideal for walking meditation. This classical seven-circuit labyrinth is located beside an Episcopal church in Marblehead, Massachusetts.

Meditation Exercise No. 10: Meditation in Action

In the walking meditation, the focus of the exercise is the movement of the arms and legs while walking. In meditation in action, the focus is whatever movement you are doing.

You can apply this awareness to eating if you want to lose weight, to sports if you want to excel in competition, or to practice if you want to master a musical instrument. An intriguing application is using meditation in action to calm the mind while doing chores such as cleaning dishes, taking out the garbage, or raking leaves.

Again, Buddhists refer to this idea as mindfulness. You can apply mindfulness by being totally aware and calmly focused on whatever you are doing, whenever you are doing it during your day.

Finding Your Path

As you explore and try paths of meditation, you will find the one that is right for you. Meditation can help you see that you are more than just your body, mind, or emotions alone. Beyond this, you are a wise, compassionate, creative being. You have been given the precious gift of life with which to experience and explore the universe. Meditation is a tool that can guide you, helping you to bring the gift of your unique self into the world.

Many books and Web sites are available to guide you on your journey. But remember, there is no substitute for learning about meditation in person from a qualified instructor. Insight meditation teacher Jack Kornfield recommends that you choose a "name brand" tradition— preferably a tradition that's been around for hundreds of years and has withstood the test of time.

41

affirmation Positive phrase.

antidote Something that relieves or counteracts.

asana Term that means steady pose; posture used in the practice of yoga.

Buddha A Sanskrit word that literally means "one who is awake." This adjective word became a way of referring to Siddhartha Gautama, the founder of Buddhism.

compassion Deep feeling of sharing the suffering of, and the inclination to give support to, another.

Dalai Lama Reincarnated spiritual and political leader of Tibet.

enlightenment For spiritual seekers, the ultimate goal. One who is enlightened experiences the essential truth of his or her life fully, and is at peace with its changes and appreciates its beauty.

Hinduism Major religion of India.

Kabbalah Mystical teachings based on Jewish scriptures.

koan A traditional riddle that a Zen teacher assigns to a student.

labyrinth Maze or winding path, often constructed in an intricate pattern.

Lama A Tibetan spiritual master.

lotus position Classical meditation posture in which the legs are crossed and the feet are brought up to rest on the inner thighs.

mantra Repetition of sounds or words to aid in meditation.

meditation A practice of cultivating calmness, alertness, and a compassionate state of mind.

mindfulness Bringing a higher level of awareness to ordinary experience while remaining natural.

mystical Mysterious; having spiritual meaning that is not obvious.

object of meditation Focus of a meditation.

rejuvenate To renew or make young again.

Rinpoche Same as Lama.

Sanskrit Classical language of India.

solace Consolation or relief from anxiety.

transcendental Supernatural, beyond the normal limits of experience.

visualization Bringing particular images to mind as part of meditation.

yoga Term that means union with the divine. A general term for the Indian practice of meditations, diet, postures, and lifestyle leading to higher states of consciousness.

Zen Branch of Buddhism practiced in Japan in which meditation is the key to achieving enlightenment.

Insight Meditation Society
1230 Pleasant Street
Barre, MA 01005
(978) 355-4378
Web site: http://www.dharma.org/ims
One of the longest established meditation societies in the West,
known for its down-to-earth style and silent meditation retreats.

San Francisco Zen Center
300 Page Street
San Francisco, CA 94102
(415) 863-3136
Web site: http://www.sfzc.org
A cornerstone of Zen Buddhism in America, this center was founded
by the great Zen master Shunryu Suzuki Roshi in 1962. The site
contains many links to Soto Zen communities.

Shambhala International
1084 Tower Road
Halifax, Nova Scotia
B3H 2Y5, Canada
(902) 425-4275
Web site: http://www.shambhala.org
An international network of meditation centers, founded by the great
Tibetan teacher Chogyam Trungpa Rinpoche. The Shambhala
Center nearest you will be a great resource as you begin on your path.

Springwater Center
7179 Mill Street
Springwater, NY 14560
(585) 669-2141

Web site: http://www.springwatercenter.org
This center was founded by Toni Packer, a former Zen Buddhist who decided to move away from the rituals of Zen practice. Here you will find a fresh and intelligent approach to the practice of meditation.

Wide Awake
Web site: http://www.wide-awake.org
This meditation site, aimed at teens, has a great events page where you can find out about retreats, workshops, and social gatherings for teens and young adults who are interested in meditation.

Web Sites

Due to the changing nature of Internet links, Rosen Publishing has developed an online list of Web sites related to the subject of this book. This site is updated regularly. Please use this link to access the list:

http://www.rosenlinks.com/tmh/medi

for further reading

Baroni, Helen J., Ph.D. *The Illustrated Encyclopedia of Zen Buddhism*. New York, NY: The Rosen Publishing Group, 2002.

Batchelor, Stephen. *Buddhism Without Beliefs*. New York, NY: Riverhead Books, 1997.

Chodron, Pema. *The Places That Scare You: A Guide to Fearlessness in Difficult Times*. Boston, MA: Shambhala Publications, 2002.

Hahn, Thich Nhat. *Anger: Wisdom for Cooling the Flames*. New York, NY: Riverhead, 2001.

Mipham Rinpoche, Sakyong. *Turning the Mind Into an Ally*. New York, NY: Riverhead, 2003.

Shunryu, Suzuki. *Zen Mind, Beginner's Mind*. New York, NY: Weatherhill, 1973.

Taylor, Rodney L., Ph.D. *The Illustrated Encyclopedia of Confucianism*. New York, NY: The Rosen Publishing Group, 2005.

A

affirmations, 31–33

B

Buddhism, 8, 18, 21–24, 28, 41

C

calming the mind, 9–10
chanting, 18–20
contemplation of kindness, 20
contemplation practice, 17

H

Hinduism, 8, 18, 21–22, 24–25, 28

J

Jackson, Phil, 34
Jung, Carl, 25

K

Kabbalah, 27
Karajan, Herbert von, 23
Kornfield, Jack, 41

M

Maharishi Yogi, 25
mantras, 18–20
meditation
    developing a practice, 10–15
    environment for, 12–13
    exercises, 9–10, 18–20, 33,
        34–39, 39–41

explanation of, 4–6
finding a comfortable position,
    13–14
misconceptions about, 7–8
myths and facts about, 28–29
solitary or group, 14–15
timekeeping during, 13
mindfulness, 6, 8, 41

N

nirvana, 23

R

retreats, 39
Rinpoche, Sogyal, 18

S

Siddhartha (the Buddha), 8–9,
    22, 29
Sufism, 27

T

Tibetan Buddhism, 23
transcendental meditation, 25

V

visualization, 9, 23

Y

yoga, 9, 13, 24–25

Z

Zen Buddhism, 13, 23, 27

About the Author

Andrew Moore began practicing and studying meditation in Austin, Texas, while in college. For the past twelve years, he has been a grateful student of Sakyong Mipham Rinpoche and Pema Chodron, American teachers who practice in the Tibetan Buddhist tradition. The author lived and studied for three years at Karmê Chöling, a Buddhist meditation retreat in northern Vermont, and a wonderful place to meditate year-round. Moore now lives in Brooklyn, New York, and is a certified meditation instructor for the New York Shambhala Center.

Photo Credits

Cover, p. 1 (top left) © www.istockphoto.com/Koch Valérie; cover, p. 1 (middle left) © www.istockphoto.com/Roman Korotaev; cover, p. 1 (bottom left) © www.istockphoto.com/Dimitry Romanchuck; cover (right) © www.istockphoto.com/Kristen Johansen; cover, pp. 1, 3 (head and brain) © www.istockphoto.com/Vasiliy Yakobchuk; p. 3 (laptop) www.istockphoto.com/Brendon De Suza; p. 3 and additional page backgrounds (books) © www.istockphoto.com/Michal Koziarski; pp. 4, 7, 17, 21, 30 (head) © www.istockphoto.com; p. 4 www.istockphoto.com/Izabela Habur; p. 5 © www.istockphoto.com/VikramRaghuvanshi; p. 7 © www.istockphoto.com/Jaroslaw Wojcik; p. 8 Dimas Ardian/Getty Images; p. 11 © www.istockphoto.com/Anna Bryukhanova; p. 12 Kaz Mori/The Image Bank/Getty Images; p. 14 John Nordell/*The Christian Science Monitor*/Getty Images; p. 17 © www.istockphoto.com/Justin Horrocks; p. 19 Paula Bronstein/Getty Images; p. 21 © www.istockphoto.com/Jacom Stephens; p. 22 © www.istockphoto.com/Martyn Unsworth; p. 24 VisionsofAmerica/Joe Sohm/The Image Bank/Getty Images; p. 25 © www.istockphoto.com/Joseph C. Justice Jr.; pp. 26, 40 © AP Images; p. 30 © www.istockphoto.com/Jacob Wackerhausen; p. 31 Christina Kennedy/DK Stock/Getty Images; p. 34 Shutterstock.com; p. 37 © www.istockphoto.com/Nicholas Monu.

Designer: Nelson Sá; Editor: Christopher Roberts
Photo Researcher: Cindy Reiman